8933

DISCARD

D1366920

KANSAS CITY PUBLIC LIBRARY

3/12

Graphic Library

When Volcanoes Erupt!

by Nel Yomtov
illustrated by Sean O'Neill

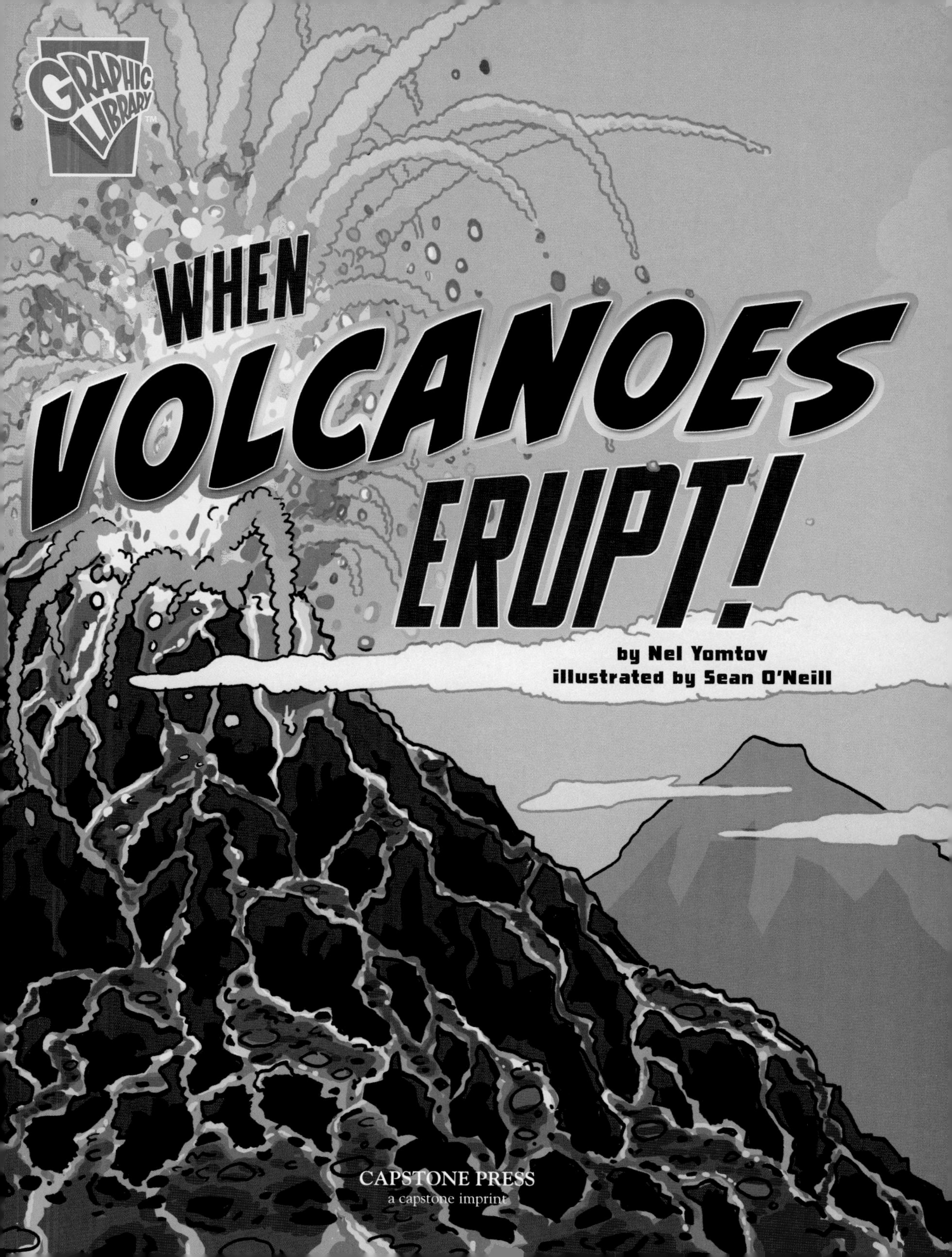

CAPSTONE PRESS
a capstone imprint

Graphic Library is published by Capstone Press,
1710 Roe Crest Drive, North Mankato, Minnesota 56003.
www.capstonepub.com

Copyright © 2012 by Capstone Press, a Capstone imprint. All rights reserved.
No part of this publication may be reproduced in whole or in part, or stored in a
retrieval system, or transmitted in any form or by any means, electronic, mechanical,
photocopying, recording, or otherwise, without written permission of the publisher.
For information regarding permission, write to Capstone Press,
1710 Roe Crest Drive, North Mankato, Minnesota 56003.

Books published by Capstone Press are manufactured with paper
containing at least 10 percent post-consumer waste.

Library of Congress Cataloging-in-Publication Data
Yomtov, Nelson.
  When volcanoes erupt! / by Nel Yomtov.
      p. cm.—(Graphic library. adventures in science)
  Includes bibliographical references and index.
  Summary: "In graphic novel format, explores volcanic eruptions, including volcano
formation, types of volcanoes, and the study of volcanoes"—Provided by publisher.
  ISBN 978-1-4296-7547-5 (library binding)
  ISBN 978-1-4296-7990-9 (paperback)
  1. Volcanoes—Juvenile literature. 2. Volcanology—Juvenile literature. I. Title. II. Series
QE521.3.Y66 2012
551.21—dc23   2011033564

Art Director
Nathan Gassman

Designer
Lori Bye

Editor
Anthony Wacholtz

Production Specialist
Laura Manthe

Consultant:
Ingrid Ukstins Peate, PhD
Assistant Professor
Geoscience Department
University of Iowa

The author wishes to dedicate this book to his brother, Barry.

Printed in the United States of America in Stevens Point, Wisconsin.
102011   006404WZS12

TABLE OF CONTENTS

CHAPTER 1

VIOLENT EARTH

On August 24, AD 79, Mount Vesuvius in Italy erupted in furious anger. In Pompeii, enormous clouds of ash fell on the city. People were buried alive.

In Herculaneum, hot gases and ash surged through the town. Traveling at speeds up to 186 miles (300 kilometers) per hour, the gases and ash destroyed everything in its path.

How are volcanoes capable of such incredible fury and destructive power?

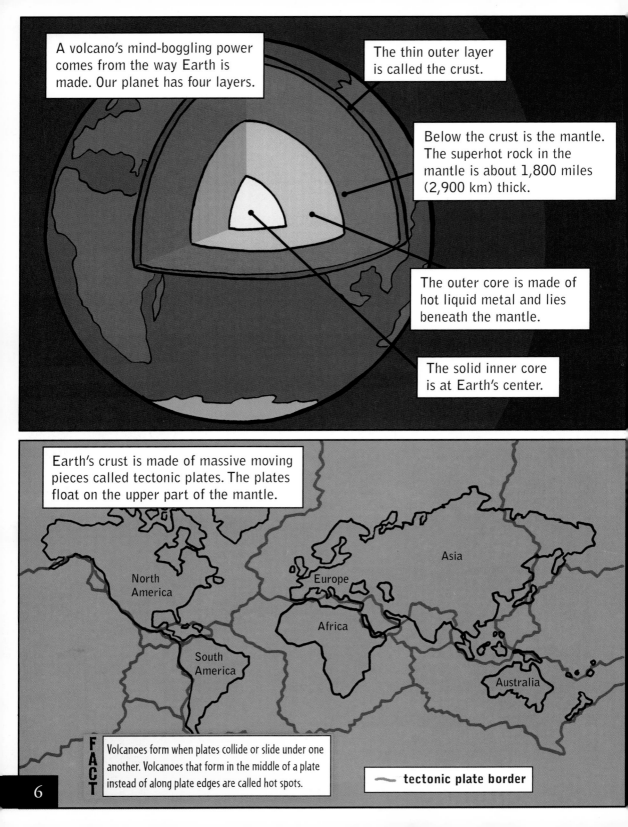

A volcano's mind-boggling power comes from the way Earth is made. Our planet has four layers.

The thin outer layer is called the crust.

Below the crust is the mantle. The superhot rock in the mantle is about 1,800 miles (2,900 km) thick.

The outer core is made of hot liquid metal and lies beneath the mantle.

The solid inner core is at Earth's center.

Earth's crust is made of massive moving pieces called tectonic plates. The plates float on the upper part of the mantle.

North America

Europe

Asia

Africa

South America

Australia

FACT Volcanoes form when plates collide or slide under one another. Volcanoes that form in the middle of a plate instead of along plate edges are called hot spots.

— **tectonic plate border**

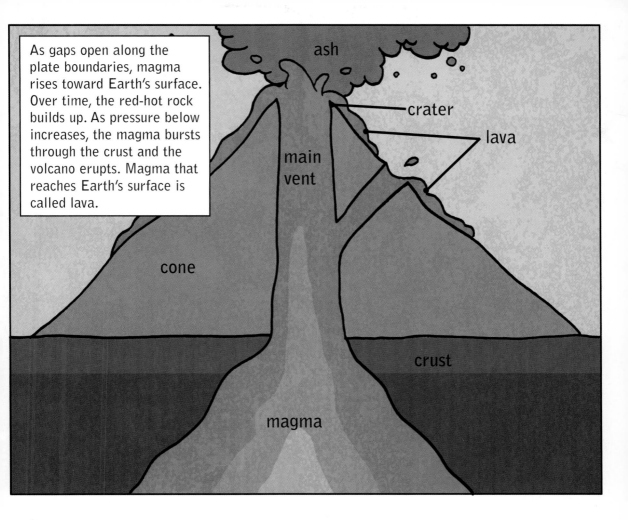

As gaps open along the plate boundaries, magma rises toward Earth's surface. Over time, the red-hot rock builds up. As pressure below increases, the magma bursts through the crust and the volcano erupts. Magma that reaches Earth's surface is called lava.

ash

crater

lava

main vent

cone

crust

magma

THE RING OF FIRE

The Ring of Fire is an area in the Pacific Ocean that has about 450 volcanoes. This area stretches for about 24,800 miles (40,000 km). Volcanoes aren't the only feature it's known for. About 90 percent of the world's earthquakes occur along the Ring of Fire.

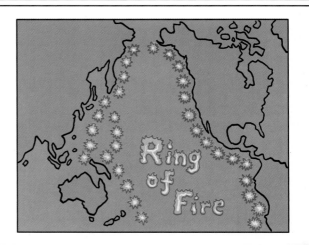

Ring of Fire

There are three main types of volcanoes: cinder cone, shield, and stratovolcano.

ACTIVE, DORMANT, OR EXTINCT

Volcanoes can be classified as active, dormant, or extinct. An active volcano, such as Mount Etna in Italy, is either erupting now or has erupted in recorded history. Dormant volcanoes are those that are not erupting but might in the future. Mauna Kea in Hawaii is a dormant volcano. Extinct volcanoes, such as Mount Kilimanjaro in Tanzania, are never expected to erupt.

A cinder cone forms from magma erupting from a single vent. The lava cools into cinders. The cinders fall around the volcano, forming a small, circular cone.

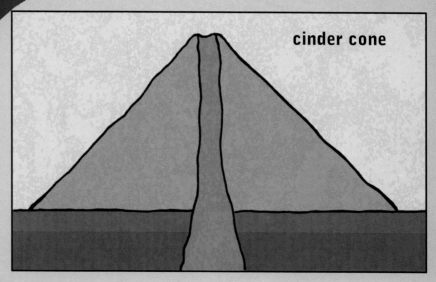

cinder cone

shield

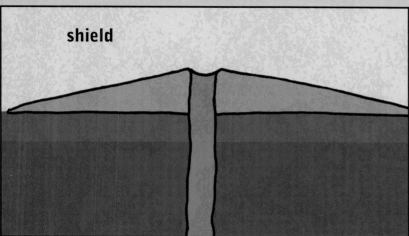

Shield volcanoes are the largest type of volcano. They form when lava gushes out of one or more vents in the volcano. The flowing lava travels long distances before it cools and hardens. As layer upon layer of lava harden, they can create a large volcano. The Mauna Loa shield volcano in Hawaii stretches 60 miles (97 km) across.

Stratovolcanoes are the most destructive types of volcanoes. They form in layers of flowing lava, volcanic ash, cinders, and bombs of lava. Stratovolcanoes have steep walls that form the cone. They are also called composite volcanoes.

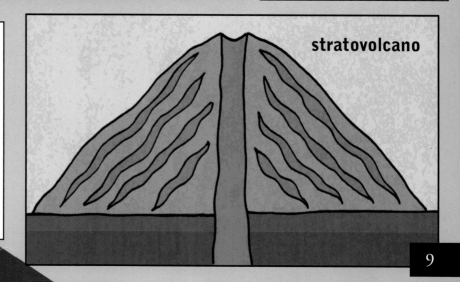

stratovolcano

CHAPTER 2

ERUPTION!

The type of volcano that forms depends on the magma and lava that reaches the surface.

Hawaiian eruption

The lava in a Hawaiian eruption is very fluid and may seep out of several vents. It travels quickly over a wide area, building up a shield volcano. Because the gases in the magma escape quickly, not much ash is formed.

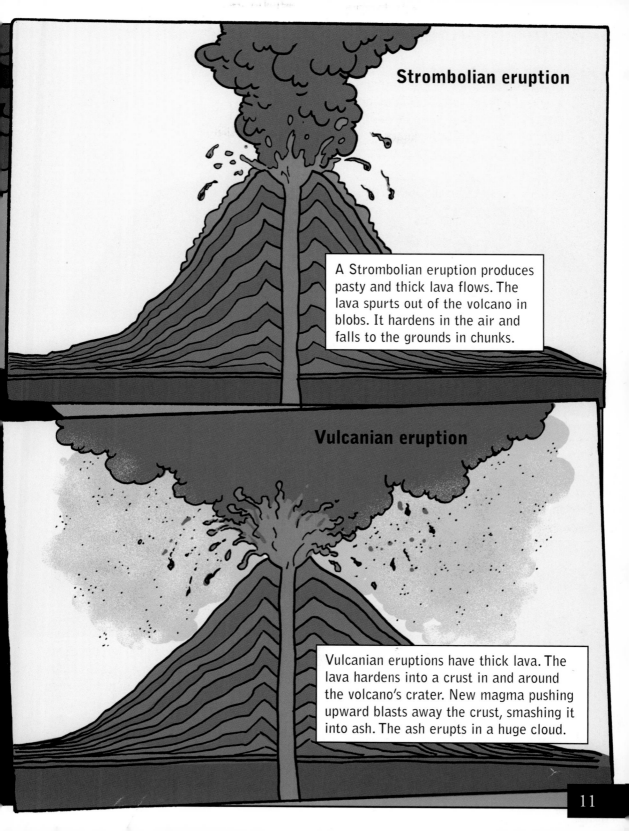

Strombolian eruption

A Strombolian eruption produces pasty and thick lava flows. The lava spurts out of the volcano in blobs. It hardens in the air and falls to the grounds in chunks.

Vulcanian eruption

Vulcanian eruptions have thick lava. The lava hardens into a crust in and around the volcano's crater. New magma pushing upward blasts away the crust, smashing it into ash. The ash erupts in a huge cloud.

Peléean eruption

In a Peléean eruption, thick magma blocks the main vent. Rising magma then pushes the blockage upward, forming a dome above ground.

FACT Peléean eruptions are named for Mount Pelée. This volcano is on the island of Martinique in the Caribbean Sea.

When pressure builds up, the dome splits open. A huge explosion follows, blasting hot gas, ash, and rock onto the volcano's sides.

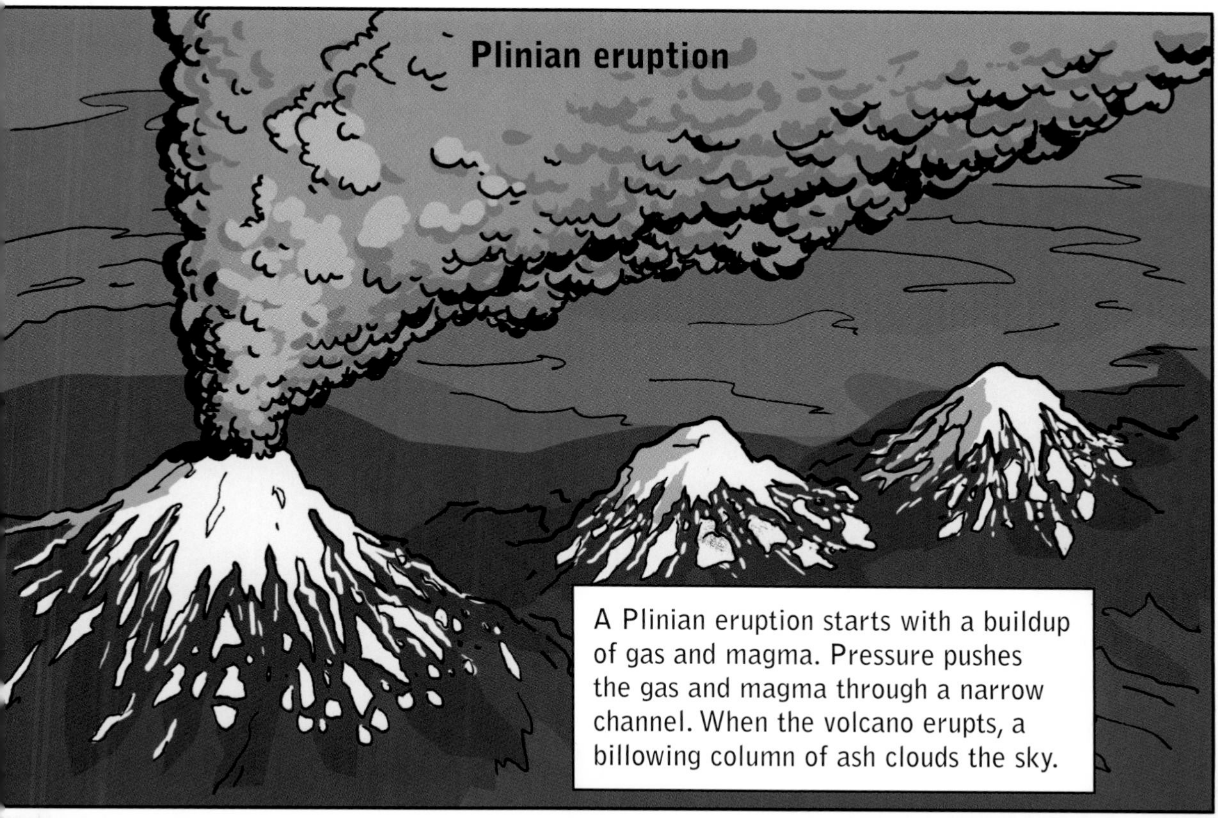
Plinian eruption
A Plinian eruption starts with a buildup of gas and magma. Pressure pushes the gas and magma through a narrow channel. When the volcano erupts, a billowing column of ash clouds the sky.

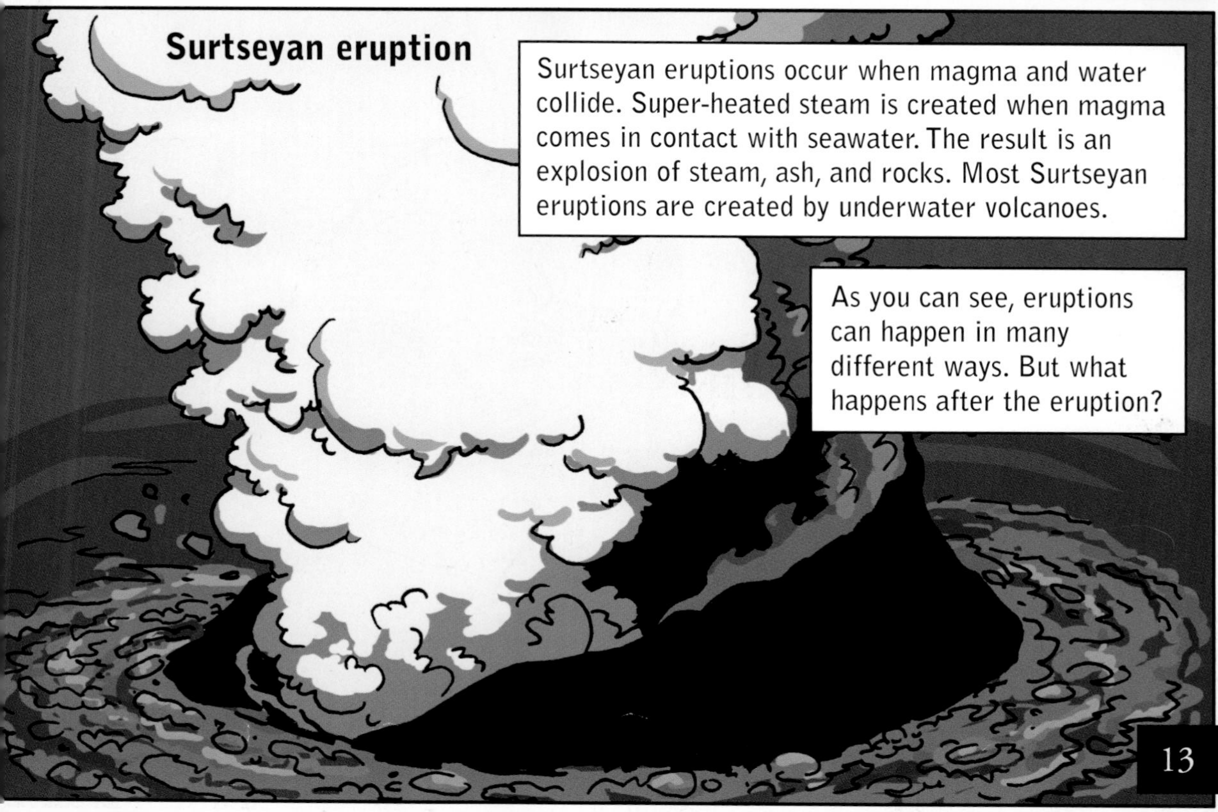
Surtseyan eruption
Surtseyan eruptions occur when magma and water collide. Super-heated steam is created when magma comes in contact with seawater. The result is an explosion of steam, ash, and rocks. Most Surtseyan eruptions are created by underwater volcanoes.
As you can see, eruptions can happen in many different ways. But what happens after the eruption?

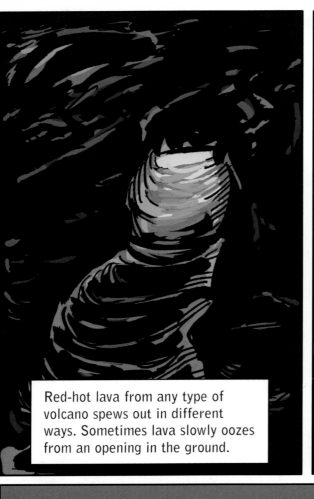

As it does, a lava flow forms. A pahoehoe flow contains liquid rock. Sometimes the hot lava oozes under the cooled, hardened surface. You could even walk across it while the lava moved beneath your feet.

Red-hot lava from any type of volcano spews out in different ways. Sometimes lava slowly oozes from an opening in the ground.

Aa flows occur when the lava begins to cool. As the lava slowly moves, it cracks apart and becomes block-like. Aa flows are sticky and can grow to be 330 feet (100 meters) thick.

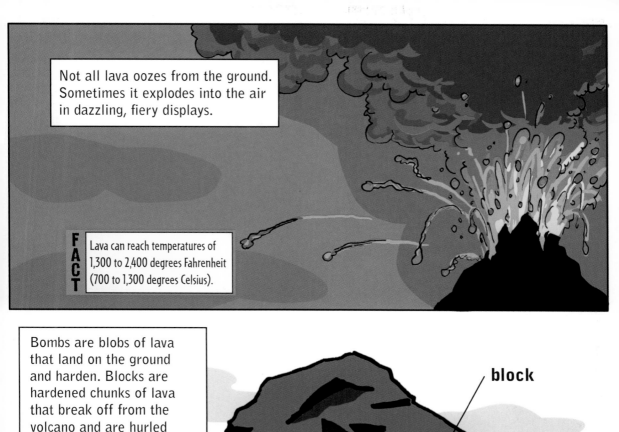

Not all lava oozes from the ground. Sometimes it explodes into the air in dazzling, fiery displays.

FACT Lava can reach temperatures of 1,300 to 2,400 degrees Fahrenheit (700 to 1,300 degrees Celsius).

Bombs are blobs of lava that land on the ground and harden. Blocks are hardened chunks of lava that break off from the volcano and are hurled skyward during an eruption.

block

As dangerous as lava can be, it is not the deadliest part of an eruption. The most feared killer of a volcanic eruption is all the ash, cinder, and gas.

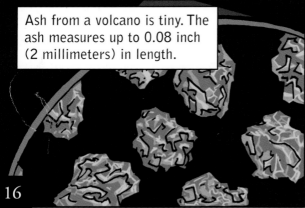

Ash from a volcano is tiny. The ash measures up to 0.08 inch (2 millimeters) in length.

Cinders are larger, measuring up to 25 inches (64 centimeters) long.

Sometimes the huge cloud of material stays close to the ground. Deadly waves of choking hot gas, pumice, and lava travel along the ground. Called pyroclastic flows, the material can travel up to 450 miles (724 km) an hour. Temperatures inside the flow can reach 800 degrees Fahrenheit (427 degrees Celsius).

Mount Pinatubo in the Philippines blew its top in 1991. It belched giant clouds of ash 21 miles (34 km) high. The clouds blocked out the sun for days. Pyroclastic flows killed more than 800 people and destroyed huge areas of farmland.

In a pyroclastic surge, the cloud of volcanic material contains a large amount of gases. The surge can move quickly up hills and ridges.

Pyroclastic falls occur when volcanic material is ejected from a volcano and falls to the ground far from the vent.

The gases in a pyroclastic flow are often highly poisonous. In 1991 an eruption of Mount Unzen in Japan released a massive cloud of gases.

The poisonous fumes killed 43 people, including two volcanologists. Survivors had trouble breathing and suffered burning pains in their eyes and noses.

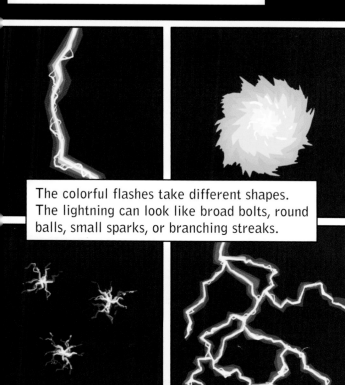

Volcanic eruptions can also cause brilliant flashes of lightning. As pieces of ash rub against each other, electrical charges create lightning flashes.

The colorful flashes take different shapes. The lightning can look like broad bolts, round balls, small sparks, or branching streaks.

FUMAROLES, HOT SPRINGS, AND GEYSERS

Volcanic activity heats water in the ground. Fumaroles are vents near a volcano through which steam escapes. A hot spring occurs when boiling water deep in the earth makes its way through cracks in the rocks above. As the hot water moves through the rocks, it cools. Then the water emerges from the ground. When hot rocks deep in the ground boil water, a geyser is formed, shooting up jets of steaming water.

The enormous power of some volcanoes can trigger natural disasters. Mudflows called lahars are destructive, moving masses of mud, sand, gravel, boulders, and water.

In 1980, a massive volcanic eruption blew out the side of Mount St. Helens in Washington. Lahars of rocks, ice, snow, dirt, and trees slid down the mountain's slope. Bridges were destroyed. The surrounding areas were buried in a layer of muck and mud 148 feet (45 m) high.

FACT Lahars can travel up to 60 miles (97 km) per hour.

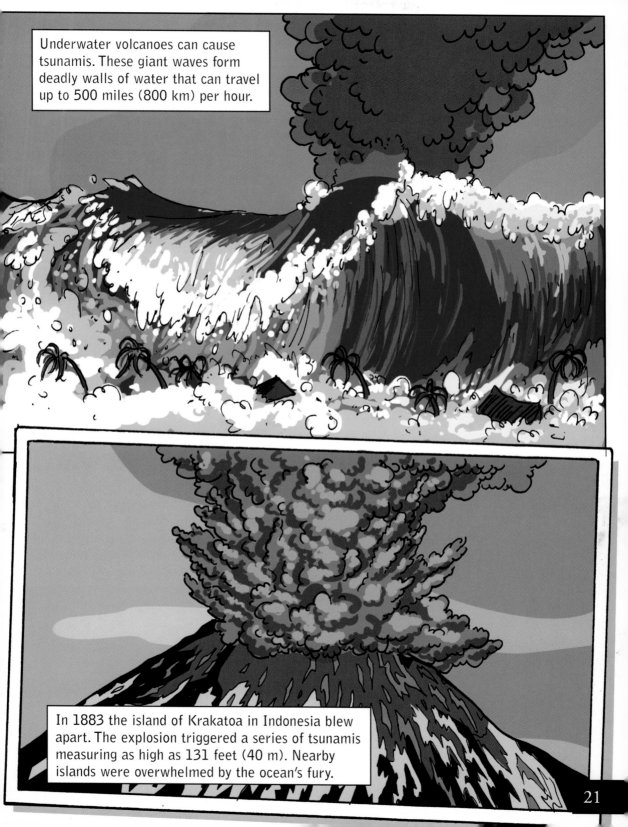

Underwater volcanoes can cause tsunamis. These giant waves form deadly walls of water that can travel up to 500 miles (800 km) per hour.

In 1883 the island of Krakatoa in Indonesia blew apart. The explosion triggered a series of tsunamis measuring as high as 131 feet (40 m). Nearby islands were overwhelmed by the ocean's fury.

CHAPTER 3

IN THE WAKE OF DISASTER

Despite their enormous destructive power, volcanoes are important to life on Earth. Some scientists believe that prehistoric volcanoes are responsible for all the water on our planet.

The water was created when volcanoes gave off steam that later became water. Volcanoes also gave off other gases that helped form our atmosphere.

HSSSSS

Many minerals and metals that are helpful to us come from volcanic activity. Hot underground water carries minerals and chemicals into cracks in the rocks. Copper, lead, zinc, and mercury are the result of underground volcanic activity.

K-CHUNK
K-CHUNK

Volcanoes also create new land. Millions of tons of lava blast out of a volcano, harden, and become land. The lava breaks down into nutrients that create rich soil for farming.

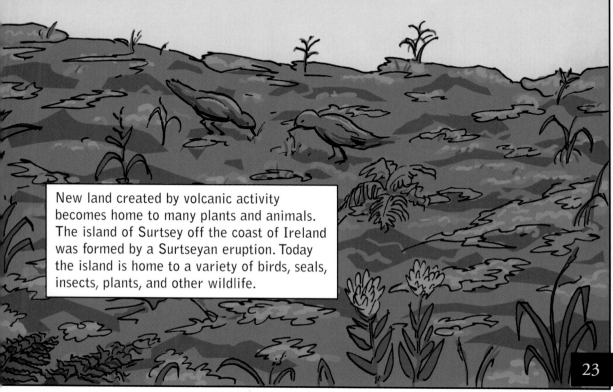

New land created by volcanic activity becomes home to many plants and animals. The island of Surtsey off the coast of Ireland was formed by a Surtseyan eruption. Today the island is home to a variety of birds, seals, insects, plants, and other wildlife.

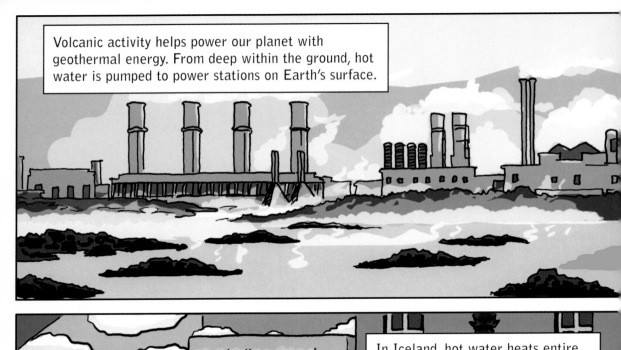

Volcanic activity helps power our planet with geothermal energy. From deep within the ground, hot water is pumped to power stations on Earth's surface.

FÖT GEYMA

matvöruverslun birgðir

In Iceland, hot water heats entire towns. Used hot water is then piped below the streets to melt snow.

The power of volcanoes is also used to help grow food in Iceland. Hot springs produce geothermal energy that powers many greenhouses.

Some power plants take steam directly from the ground to spin turbines. When the turbines spin, they make electricity.

VOLCANIC BEAUTY

Volcanic eruptions can affect the appearance of the sun and moon. Ash and volcanic gas in the atmosphere let in some of the sun's rays and bounce back others. The results are sunsets and sunrises of breathtaking colors.

CHAPTER 4 STUDYING AND PREDICTING VOLCANOES

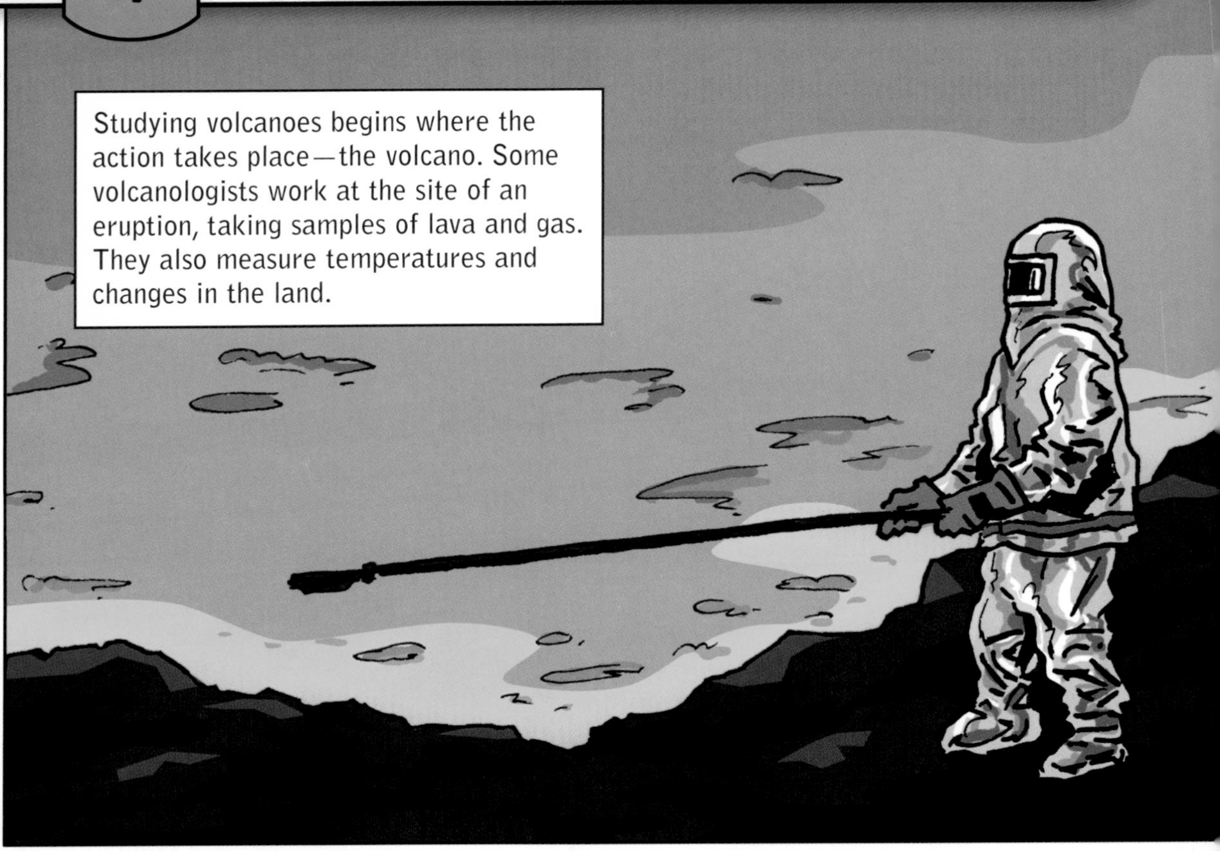
Studying volcanoes begins where the action takes place—the volcano. Some volcanologists work at the site of an eruption, taking samples of lava and gas. They also measure temperatures and changes in the land.

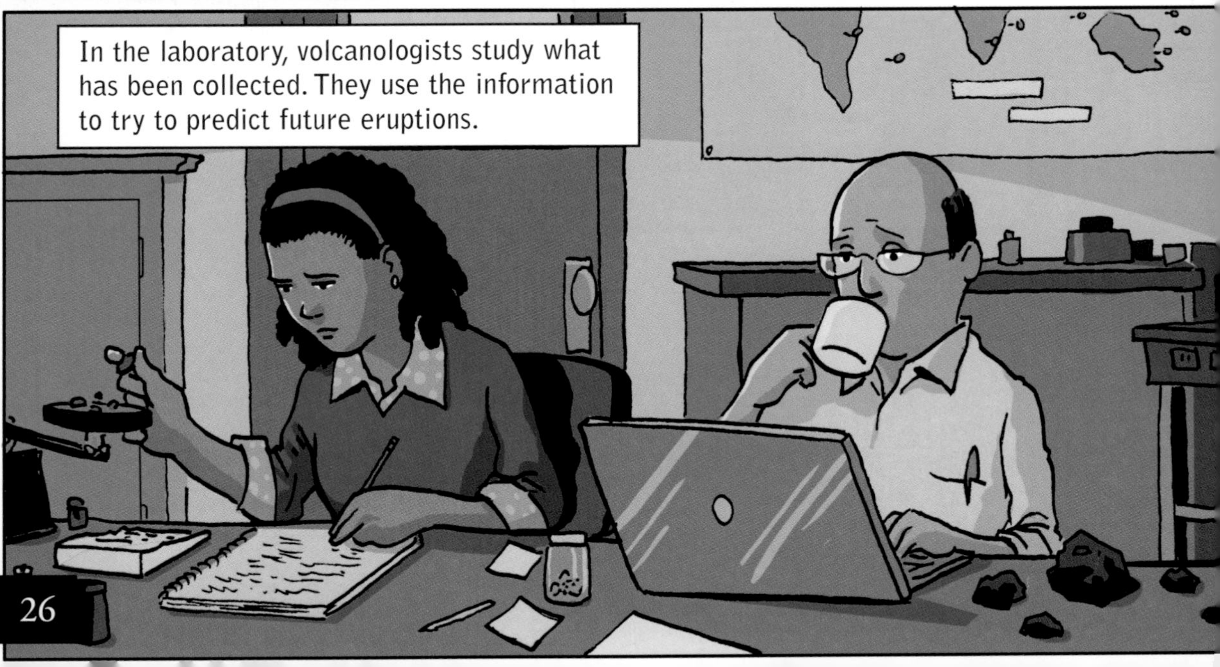
In the laboratory, volcanologists study what has been collected. They use the information to try to predict future eruptions.

Researchers use seismographs to record a volcano's activity. Seismographs record earthquake activity that could lead to an eruption. The machines are placed around the volcano to get readings from several different areas.

Volcanologists use tiltmeters to measure changes in the ground surface near the volcano. This helps volcanologists know if pressure, cracks, gases, or lava are forming beneath the earth.

Volcanologists also take samples of gases near the volcano. Studying the samples helps scientists know which gases are present and where they are coming from.

It's impossible to prevent a volcanic eruption. But knowing when one will happen can save lives. Scientists can alert government officials and the public of a possible eruption. People are often evacuated from the area.

The U.S. Federal Emergency Management Agency has tips for people living near a volcano. Wear long-sleeved shirts, pants, and a dust mask. Follow evacuation orders by local officials.

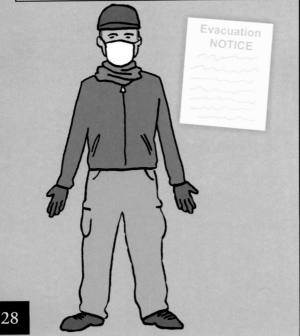

Evacuation
NOTICE

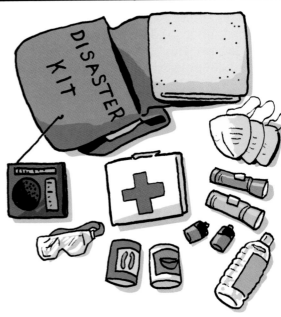

DISASTER KIT

You should also have a disaster kit prepared. It should include a first-aid kit, a radio, flashlights, batteries, blankets, goggles, and breathing masks. Dried or canned food and water are important in case you are trapped.

Since the beginning of time, volcanoes have shaped our planet. They helped create the air we breathe and the water we use. They enrich the soil and create new landmasses for life to thrive upon.

Yet they are capable of causing immense destruction. Volcanoes are truly one of nature's most powerful and feared forces.

GLOSSARY

aa (AH-AH)—a type of lava that has a rough, angular surface

active (AK-tiv)—a volcano that is erupting or has erupted in recorded history

ash (ASH)—fine particles formed in explosive eruptions that measure up to 0.08 inches (2 mm)

cinder (SIN-duhr)—a pyroclastic fragment that measures up to 2 inches (5 cm)

crater (KRA-turh)—a bowl-shaped depression in the top of a volcanic cone

dormant (DOR-muhnt)—a volcano that is not presently erupting but may do so in the future

dust (DUST)—the tiniest particles of volcanic ash

extinct (ek-STINGKT)—a volcano that is not erupting and is not expected to in the future

lahar (la-HAR)—a volcanic mudflow

lava (LA-vuh)—magma that has reached the surface

magma (MAG-muh)—melted, or molten, rock beneath the surface of the earth

pahoehoe (pay-HOY-hoy)—a liquidy type of lava with a smooth surface

vent (VENT)—an opening in a volcano through which volcanic material is ejected

READ MORE

Fradin, Judy, and Dennis Fradin. *Volcano!* National Geographic Kids. Washington, D.C.: National Geographic, 2010.

Harbo, Christopher. *The Explosive World of Volcanoes with Max Axiom Super Scientist.* Graphic Science. Mankato, Minn.: Capstone Press, 2008.

Rubin, Ken. *Volcanoes and Earthquakes.* Insiders. New York: Simon & Schuster Books for Young Readers, 2007.

Van Rose, Susanna. *Volcanoes & Earthquakes.* Eyewitness Books. New York: DK Publishing, 2008.

INTERNET SITES

FactHound offers a safe, fun way to find Internet sites related to this book. All of the sites on FactHound have been researched by our staff.

Here's all you do:

Visit *www.facthound.com*

Type in this code: 9781429675475

Check out projects, games and lots more at
www.capstonekids.com

INDEX